A Closer Walk
A Closer Talk

A Closer Walk
A Closer Talk

Prayer As A Way Of Life

R. A. TORREY   C. H. SPURGEON   BILLY SUNDAY
D. L. MOODY AND E. M. BOUNDS

Ambassador

A CLOSER WALK, A CLOSER TALK

AMBASSADOR PRODUCTIONS LTD
PROVIDENCE HOUSE
16 Hillview Avenue,
Belfast,
U.K., BT5 6JR

37 Leconfield Road,
Loughborough,
Leics.
U.K., LE11 3SP

ISBN 0 907927 55 6

Printed at the Press of the Publishers

Contents

Introduction

Prayer is one of the greatest privileges known to man. The fact that mere mortals can actually speak to the God who created and sustains all things is amazing, even mysterious. Yet it is true.

Prayer is also one of the greatest war zones for the believer. It is while we are in prayer that the devil fears us most and he will use any method to dissuade us from praying. After all it is the means for the soldier to maintain contact with general headquarters! That is one reason, for instance, why we find it so hard to concentrate while praying. Thought after thought floods our mind, not necessarily wrong or improper thoughts, just anything but the matter in hand. accordingly prayer can become one of the most neglected areas of our Christian lives. Having tried and tried in vain we sometimes tend to just give up until our consciences smite us again and so, back to the battle.

It is this very struggle, which every Christian faces, that makes books on prayer both necessary and valuable. They tend to motivate and stimulate us to pray and that has to be good.

In this book there are gathered the thoughts of some of God's greatest warriors on the theme of prayer. Each representing a different point on the Christian spectrum they tackle the bedrock issues concerning prayer. They are all men who have experienced the same dilemmas that we face and learned how to win.

Their experience together with their study of the subject make their conclusions compulsive and vital reading for those who wish to be overcomers in the arena of prayer.

1

The Importance of Prayer

R. A. TORREY

In Ephesians 6:18 we read words which put the tremendous importance of prayer with startling and overwhelming force:

'Praying always with all prayer and supplication in the Spirit, and watching thereunto with all perseverance and supplication for all saints.'

When we stop to weigh the meaning of these words, then note the connection in which they are found, the intelligent child of God is driven to say, I must pray, pray, pray. I must put all my energy, all my heart into prayer. Whatever else I do, I must pray.'

'With all prayer and supplication praying at all seasons in the spirit, and watching thereunto in all perseverance and supplication for all the saints.'

Note the *alls*: 'with *all* prayer,' 'at *all* seasons,' 'in *all* perseverance,' 'for *all* the saints.' Note once more the strong expression, 'watching thereunto,' more literally, 'being sleepless thereunto.' Paul realised the natural sloth-fulness of man, especially his natural slothfulness in prayer.

How seldom we pray things through! How often the church and the individual get right up to the verge of a great blessing in prayer and just then let go, get drowsy, and quit. I wish that these words, 'being sleepless unto prayer,' might burn into our hearts. I wish the whole verse might burn into our hearts.

But why is this constant, persistent, sleepless, overcoming prayer so needful?

1. Because there is a Devil.

He is cunning, he is mighty, he never rests, he is ever plotting the downfall of the child of God; and if we relax in prayer, the Devil will succeed in ensnaring us.

This is the thought of the context. Verse 12 reads:

'For our wrestling is not against flesh and blood, but against the principalities, against the powers, against the world rulers of this darkness, against the spiritual hosts of wickedness in the heavenly places.'

Then comes verse 13:

'Wherefore take up the whole armour of God, that ye may be able to withstand in the evil day, and, having done all , to stand.'

Next follows a description of the different parts of the Christian's armour which we are to put on if we are to stand against the Devil and his mighty wiles. Then Paul brings all to a climax in verse 18, telling us that to all else we must add prayer - constant, persistent, untiring, sleepless prayer in the Holy Spirit, or all else will go for nothing.

2. Prayer is God's appointed way for obtaining things, and the great secret of all lack in our experience, in our life, and in our work is neglect of prayer.

James brings this out very forcibly in chapter 4 and verse 2 of his epistle; 'Ye have not because ye ask not.' These words contain the secret of the poverty and powerlessness of the average Christian - neglect of prayer.

Many a Christian is asking, 'Why is it I make so little progress in my Christian life?' 'Neglect of prayer,' God answers. 'You have not because you ask not.'

Many a minister is asking, 'Why is it I see so little fruit from my labours?' Again God answers, 'Neglect of prayer. You have not because you ask not.'

Many a Sunday school teacher is asking, 'Why is it that I see so few converted in my Sunday school class?' Still God answers, 'Neglect of prayer. You have not because you ask not.'

Both ministers and churches are asking, 'Why is it that the church of Christ makes so little headway against unbelief and error and sin and worldliness?' Once more we hear God answering, 'Neglect of prayer. You have not because you ask not.'

3. Those whom God set forth as a pattern of what he expected Christians to be - the apostles - regarded prayer as their most important business.

When the multiplying responsibilities of the early church crowded in upon them, they

'... called the multitude of the disciples unto them, and said, It is not reason that we should leave the word of God, and serve tables. Wherefore, brethren, look ye out among you seven men of honest report, full of the Holy Ghost and wisdom, whom we may appoint over this business. But we will give ourselves continually to prayer and to the ministry of the word.'

It is evident from what Paul wrote to the churches and to individuals about praying for them that much of his time, strength and thought was given to prayer (Rom. 1:9; Eph. 1:15, 16; Col. 1:9; I Thess. 3:10; II Tim. 1:3).

All the mighty men of God outside the Bible have been men of prayer. They have differed from one another in many things, but in this they have been alike.

4. Prayer occupied a very prominent place and played a very important part in the earthly life of our Lord.

Turn, for example, to Mark 1:35.

'And in the morning, rising up a great while before day, he went out, and departed into a solitary place, and there prayed.'

The preceding day had been a very busy and exciting one, but Jesus shortened the hours of needed sleep that He might arise early and give Himself to more sorely needed prayer.

Turn again to Luke 6:12, where we read,

'And it came to pass in those days that he went out into a mountain to pray, and continued all night in prayer to God.'

Our Saviour found it necessary on occasion to take a whole night for prayer.

The words 'pray' and 'prayer' are used at least twenty-five times in connection with our Lord in the brief record of His life in the four Gospels, and His praying is mentioned in places where the words are not used. Evidently prayer took much of the time and strength of Jesus. A man or woman who does not spend much time in prayer cannot properly be called a follower of Jesus Christ.

5. Praying is the most important part of the present ministry of our risen Lord. This reason for constant, persistent, sleepless, overcoming prayer seems, if possible, even more forcible.

Christ's ministry did not close with His death. His atoning work was finished then, but when He rose and ascended to the right hand of the Father, He entered upon other work for us just as important in its place as His atoning work. It cannot be divorced from His atoning work; it rests upon that as its basis, but it is necessary to our complete salvation. What that great present work is, by which He carries out salvation on to completeness, we read in Hebrews 7:25:

'Wherefore he is able also to save them to the uttermost that come unto God by him, seeing he ever liveth to make intercession for them.'

This verse tells us that Jesus is able to save us unto the uttermost, not merely *from* the uttermost, but *unto* the uttermost, unto entire completeness, absolute perfection, because He not merely died, but because He also 'ever liveth.'

The verse also tells us for what purpose He now lives, 'to make intercession for us,' to pray. Praying is the principal thing He is doing in these days. It is by His prayers that He is saving us.

The same thought is found in Paul's remarkable triumphant challenge in Romans 8:34:

'Who is he that shall condemn? It is Christ Jesus that died, yea rather, that was raised from the dead, who is at the right hand of God, who also maketh intercession for us.'

If we then are to have fellowship with Jesus Christ in His present work, we must spend much time in prayer; we must give ourselves to earnest, constant, persistent, sleepless, overcoming prayer.

I know of nothing that has so impressed me with a sense of the importance of praying at all seasons, being much and constantly in prayer, as the thought that that is the principal occupation at the present of my risen Lord. I want to have fellowship with Him, and to that end I have asked the Father whatever else He may make me, to make me an intercessor, to make me one who knows how to pray and who spends much time in prayer.

This ministry of intercession is a glorious and a mighty ministry, and we can all have part in it. The man or woman shut away from the public meeting by sickness can have part in it. The busy mother; the woman who has to take in washing for a living can have part - she can mingle prayers, for the saints and for her pastor and for the unsaved and for foreign missionaries, with the soap and water as she bends over the washtub and not do the washing any more poorly on that account. The hard-driven man of business can have part in it, praying as he hurries from duty to duty.

But of course we must, if we would maintain this spirit of constant prayer, take time - and take plenty of it - when we shall shut ourselves up in the secret place alone with God for nothing but prayer.

6. Prayer is the means that God has appointed for our receiving mercy and obtaining grace to help in time of need.

Hebrews 4:16 is one of the simplest and sweetest verses in the Bible,

'Let us therefore come boldly unto the throne of grace, that we may obtain mercy, and find grace to help in time of need.'

These words make it very plain that God has appointed a way by which we shall seek and obtain mercy and grace. That way is prayer, bold, confident, outspoken approach to the throne of grace, the most holy place of God's presence, where our sympathizing High Priest has entered in our behalf (vss. 14,15).

Mercy is what we need, grace is what we must have, or all our life and effort will end in complete failure. Prayer is the way to get them. There is infinite grace at our disposal, and we make it ours experimentally by prayer.

Oh, if we only realised the fullness of God's grace that is ours for the asking, its height and depth and length and breadth, I am sure that we would spend more time in prayer. The measure of our appropriation of grace is determined by the measure of our prayers.

Who does not feel a need for more grace? Then ask for it. Be constant and persistent in your asking. Be importunate and untiring in your asking. God delights to have us 'shameless' beggars in this direction, for it shows our faith in Him. He is mightily pleased with faith. Because of our 'shamelessness,' He will rise and give us as much as we need (Luke 11:8). What little streams of mercy and grace most of us know, when we might know rivers overflowing their banks!

7. Prayer in the name of Jesus Christ is the way Jesus Christ Himself has appointed for His disciples to obtain fullness of joy.

He states this simply and beautifully in John 16:24:

'Hitherto have ye asked nothing in my name; ask, and ye shall receive, that your joy may be fulfilled.'

'Made full' is the way the American Revised Version reads. Who is there that does not wish his joy filled full? Well, the way to have it filled full is by praying in the name of Jesus.

We all know people whose joy is filled full; indeed, it is just running over, shining from their eyes, bubbling out of their very lips, and running off their fingertips when they shake hands with you. Coming in contact with them is like coming in contact with an electrical machine charged with gladness. Now people of that sort spend much time in prayer.

Why is it that prayer in the name of Christ brings such fullness of joy? In part, because we get what we ask. But that is not the only reason, nor the greatest. It makes God real. When we ask something definite of God and He gives it, how real He becomes! He is right there! It is blessed to have a God who is real, and not merely an idea.

I remember how once I was taken suddenly and seriously sick all alone in my study. I dropped upon my knees and cried to God for help. Instantly all pain left me - I was perfectly well. It seemed as if God stood right there and had put out His hand and touched me. The joy of the healing was not so great as the joy of meeting God.

There is no greater joy on earth or in Heaven than communion with God, and prayer in the name of Jesus brings us into communion with Him. The psalmist was surely not speaking only of future blessedness but also of present blessedness when he said, 'In thy presence is fullness of joy' (Ps. 16:11). Oh, the unutterable joy of those moments when in our prayers we really press into the presence of God!

Does someone say, 'I have never known any such joy as that in prayer'? Do you take enough leisure for prayer to actually get into God's presence? Do you really give yourself up to prayer in the time which you do take?

8. Prayer, in every care and anxiety and need of life, with thanksgiving, is the means that God has appointed for our obtaining freedom from all anxiety, and the peace of God which passeth all understanding.

Paul says,

Be careful for nothing, but in everything by prayer and supplication with thanksgiving let your requests be made known unto God, and the peace of God which passeth all understanding, shall keep your hearts and minds through Christ Jesus.' Phil. 4:6,7.

To many this seems, at first glance, the picture of a beautiful life but beyond the reach of ordinary mortals. Not so at all. The verse tells us how the life is attainable by every child of God.

'Be careful for nothing,' or as the Revised Version reads, 'In nothing be anxious.' The remainder of the verse tells us how, and it is very simple: 'But in every thing by prayer and supplication with thanksgiving let your requests be made known unto God.'

What could be plainer or more simple than that? Just keep in constant touch with God, and when any trouble or vexation, great or small, comes up, speak to Him about it, never forgetting to return thanks for what He has already done. What will the result be? The peace of God which passeth all understanding shall guard your hearts and your thoughts in Christ Jesus.

That is glorious, and as simple as it is glorious! Thank God, many are trying it. Don't you know anyone who is always serene? Perhaps he is a very stormy man by his natural makeup; but troubles, conflicts, reverses and bereavements may sweep around him; yet the peace of God which passes all understanding guards his heart and thoughts in Christ Jesus.

We all know such persons. How do they manage it? Just by prayer, that is all. Those who know the deep peace of God, the unfathomable peace that passes all understanding, are always men and women of much prayer.

Some of us let the hurry of our lives crowd prayer out, and what a waste of time and energy and nerve force there is by the constant worry! One night of prayer will save us from many nights of insomnia. Time spent in prayer is not wasted, but time invested at big interest.

18

9. Prayer is the method that God Himself has appointed for our obtaining the Holy Spirit.

Upon this point the Bible is very plain. Jesus says:

'If ye then, being evil, know how to give good gifts unto your children, how much more shall your heavenly Father give the Holy Spirit to them that ask him?' Luke 11:13.

Men are telling us in these days, very good men too, 'You must not pray for the Holy Spirit.' But what are they going to do with the plain statement of Jesus Christ, 'How much more will your heavenly Father give the Holy Spirit *to them that ask him?'*

Some years ago when an address on the baptism with the Holy Spirit was announced, a brother came to me before the address and said with much feeling, 'Be sure and tell them not to pray for the Holy Spirit.'

'I will surely not tell them that, for Jesus says, 'How much more shall your heavenly Father give the Holy Spirit to them that ask him?''

'Oh, yes,' he replied, 'but that was before Pentecost.'

'How about Acts 4:31? Was that before Pentecost, or after?' I asked.

'After, of course.'

I said, 'Read it. 'And when *they had prayed*, the place was shaken where they were assembled together; and they were all *filled with the Holy Ghost*, and they spake the word of God with boldness.''

Then I asked, 'How about Acts 8:15? Was that before Pentecost or after?'

'After,' he replied.

'Please read.' 'Who, when they were come down, *prayed*

19

for them, that they might receive the Holy Ghost.''

He made no answer. What could he answer? It is plain as day in the Word of God that before Pentecost and after, the first baptism and the subsequent fillings with the Holy Spirit were received in answer to definite prayer. Experience also teaches this.

Doubtless many have received the Holy Spirit the moment of their surrender to God before there was time to pray; but how many there are who know that their first definite baptism with the Holy Spirit came while they were on their knees of faces before God, alone or in company with others, and who again and again since that have been filled with the Holy Spirit in the place of prayer!

I know this as definitely as I know that my thirst has been quenched while I was drinking water.

Early one morning in the Chicago Avenue Church prayer room where several hundred people had been assembled a number of hours in prayer, the Holy Spirit fell so manifestly, and the whole place was so filled with His presence that no one could speak or pray: only sobs of joy filled the place. men went out of that room to different parts of the country, taking trains that very morning. Reports soon came back of the outpouring of God's Holy Spirit in answer to prayer. Others went out into the city with the blessing of God upon them. This is only one instance among many that might be cited from personal experience.

If we would only spend more time in prayer, there would be more fullness of the Spirit's power in our work. Many and many a man who once worked unmistakably in the power of the Holy Spirit is now filling the air with empty shoutings, and beating it with his meaningless gesticulations, because he has let prayer be crowded out. We must spend much time on our knees before God, if we are to continue in the power of the Holy Spirit.

10. Prayer is the means that Christ has appointed whereby our hearts shall not become overcharged with surfeiting and drunkenness and cares of this life, and so the day of Christ's return come upon us suddenly as a snare.

Once of the most interesting and solemn passages upon prayer in the Bible is along this line.

'Take heed to yourselves, lest at any time your hearts be overcharged with surfeiting and drunkenness and cares of this life, and so that day come upon you unawares. For as a snare shall it come on all them that dwell on the face of the whole earth. Watch ye therefore, and pray always, that ye may be accounted worthy to escape all these things that shall come to pass, and to stand before the Son of man.' Luke 21:34-36.

According to this passage there is only one way in which we can be prepared for the coming of the Lord when He appears, that is, through much prayer.

The coming again of Jesus Christ is a subject that is awakening much interest and much discussion in our day; but it is one thing to be interested in the Lord's return and to talk about it, and quite another thing to be prepared for it. We live in an atmosphere that has a constant tendency to unfit us for Christ's coming. The world tends to draw us down by its gratifications and by its cares. There is only one way by which we can rise triumphant above these things - by constant watching unto prayer, that is, by sleeplessness unto prayer.

21

Watch in this passage is the same strong word used in Ephesians 6:18, and *always* the same strong phrase in *every season*. The man who spends little time in prayer, who is not steadfast and constant in prayer will not be ready for the Lord when He comes. But we may be ready. How? Pray! Pray! Pray!

11. Because of what prayer accomplishes.

Much has really been said upon that already, but there is much also that should be added.

(a) Prayer promotes our spiritual growth as almost nothing else, indeed as nothing else but Bible study; and true prayer and true Bible study go hand in hand.

It is through prayer that my most hidden sin is brought to light. As I kneel before God and pray, 'Search me, O God, and know my heart: try me, and know my thoughts; and see if there be any wicked way in me,' God shoots the penetrating rays of His light into the innermost recesses of my heart, causing the sins I never suspected to be brought to view.

In answer to prayer, God washes me from mine iniquity and cleanses me from my sin (Ps. 51:2).

In answer to prayer, my eyes are opened to behold wondrous things out of God's Word (Ps. 119:18).

In answer to prayer, I get wisdom to know God's way (James 1:5) and strength to walk in it.

As I meet God in prayer and gaze into His face, I am changed into His own image from glory to glory (II Cor. 3:18). Each day of true prayer life finds me more like unto my glorious Lord.

John Welch, son-in-law to John Knox, was one of the most faithful men of prayer this world ever saw. He counted that day ill spent in which seven or eight hours were not used alone with God in prayer and study of His Word. An old man speaking of him after his death said, 'He was a type of Christ.'

How came he to be so like his Master? His prayer life explains the mystery.

(b) Prayer brings power into our work. If we wish power for any work to which God calls us, be it preaching, teaching, personal work, or the rearing of our children, we can get it by earnest prayer.

A woman with a little boy who was perfectly incorrigible once came to me in desperation and said, 'What shall I do with him?'

I asked, 'Have you ever tried prayer?'

She said she thought she had prayed for him. I asked if she had made his conversion and his character a matter of definite, expectant prayer. She replied that she had not been definite in the matter. She began that day, and at once there was a marked change in the child. He grew up into Christian manhood.

How many a Sunday school teacher has taught for months and years and seen no real fruit from his labours, then has learned the secret of intercession! By earnest pleading with God, he has seen his scholars brought one by one to Christ! How many a poor preacher has become a mighty man of God by casting away his confidence in his own ability and gifts and giving himself up to God to wait upon Him for the power that comes from on High!

John Livingstone spent a night, with some likeminded, in prayer to God and religious conversation. Then when he preached the next day in the Kirk of Shotts, five hundred people were converted, or dated some definite uplift in their life to that occasion. Prayer and power are inseparable.

(c) Prayer avails for the conversion of others.

There are few converted in this world unless in connection with someone's prayers. I formerly thought that no human being had anything to do with my own conversion, for I was not converted in church or Sunday school or in personal conversation with anyone. I was awakened in the middle of the night and converted.

As far as I can remember, I had not the slightest thought of being converted or anything of that character when I went to bed and fell asleep; but I was awakened in the middle of the night and converted probably inside of five minutes. A few minutes before I was about as near eternal perdition as one gets. I had one foot over the brink and was trying to get the other one over.

I say, I thought no human being had anything to do with it, but I had forgotten my mother's prayers. And I afterwards learned that one of my college classmates had chosen me as one to pray for until I was saved.

Prayer often avails where everything else fails. By prayer the bitterest enemies of the Gospel have become its most valiant defenders; the greatest scoundrels, the truest sons of God; the vilest women, the purest saints. Oh, the power of prayer to reach down, down, down where hope itself seems vain, and lift men and women up, up, up into fellowship with and likeness to God! It is simply wonderful! How little we appreciate this marvellous weapon!

(d) Prayer brings blessings to the church.

The history of the church has always been a history of grave difficulties to overcome. The Devil hates the church and seeks in every way to block its progress; now by false doctrine, again by division, again by inward corruption of life. But by prayer, a clear way can be made through everything.

Prayer will root out heresy, allay misunderstanding, sweep away jealousies and animosities, obliterate immoralities, and bring in the full tide of God's reviving grace. History abundantly proves this. In the hour of darkest portent, when the case of the church, local or universal, has seemed beyond hope, believing men and believing women have met together and cried to God and the answer has come.

It was so in the days of Knox; it was so in the days of Wesley and Whitefield; it was so in the days of Edwards and Brainerd; it was so in the days of Finney; it was so in the days of the great revival of 1857 in this country and of 1859 in Ireland. And it will be so again in your day and mine!

Satan has marshalled his forces. Christian Science with its false Christ - a woman - lifts high its head. Others making great pretensions of apostolic methods, but covering the rankest dishonesty and hypocrisy with these pretensions, speak with loud assurance.

Christians equally loyal to the great fundamental truths of the Gospel are glowering at one another with a Devil-sent suspicion. The world, the flesh and the Devil are holding high carnival. It is now a dark day. *But* - now 'it is time for thee, Lord, to work; for they have made void thy law' (Ps. 119:126). And He is getting ready to work, and now He is listening for the voice of prayer. Will He hear it? Will He hear it from you? Will He hear it from the church as a body? I believe He will.

2

The Key Of Prayer

CHARLES H. SPURGEON

'Call unto me, and I will answer thee, and shew thee great and mighty things, which thou knowest not.' Jer. 33:3.

Some of the most learned works in the world smell of the midnight oil; but the most spiritual and most comforting books and sayings of men usually have a savour about them of prison-damp. I might quote many instances: John Bunyan's *Pilgrim* may suffice instead of a hundred others; and this good text of ours, all mouldy and chill with the prison in which Jeremiah lay, hath nevertheless a brightness and a beauty about it which it might never have had if it had not come as a cheering word to the prisoner of the Lord, shut up in the court of the prison house.

God's people have always in the worst condition found out the best of their God. He is good at all times; but He seemeth to be at His best when they are at their worst.

Rutherford had a quaint saying that when he was cast into the cellars of affliction, he remembered that the great King always kept his wine there, and he began to seek at once for the wine bottles and to drink of the 'wines on the lees well refined.'

They who dive in the sea of affliction bring up rare pearls. You know, my companions in affliction, that it is so. You have proved that He is a faithful God, and that as your tribulations abound, so your consolations also may abound by Christ Jesus.

My prayer is, in taking this text this morning, that some other prisoners of the Lord may have its joyous promise spoken home to them; that you who are straitly shut up and cannot come forth by reason of present heaviness of spirit, may hear Him say, as with a soft whisper in your ears and in your hearts, 'Call unto me, and I will answer thee, and shew thee great and mighty things, which thou knowest not.'

The text naturally splits itself up into three distinct particles of truth. Upon these let us speak as we are enabled by God the Holy Spirit. *First*, prayer commanded - 'Call unto me'; *second*, an answer promised - 'And I will answer thee'; *third*, faith encouraged - 'And shew thee great and mighty things, which thou knowest not.'

I. PRAYER COMMANDED

We are not merely counselled and recommended to pray, but bidden to pray. This is great condescension.

A hospital is built. It is considered sufficient that free admission shall be given to the sick when they seek it, but no order in council is made that a man *must* enter its gates.

A soup kitchen is well provided for in the depth of winter. Notice is promulgated that those who are poor may receive food on application; but no one thinks of passing an Act of Parliament compelling the poor to come and wait at the

28

door to take the charity. It is thought to be enough to proffer it without issuing any sort of mandate that men *shall* accept it.

Yet so strange is the *infatuation of man* on the one hand, which makes him need a command to be merciful to his own soul, and so marvellous is the condescension of our gracious God on the other, that He issues a command of love without which not a man of Adam born would partake of the gospel feast, but would rather starve than come.

We Need the Command to Pray Because of Worldliness, Sin and Unbelief

In the matter of prayer, it is even so. God's own people need, or else they would not receive it, a command to pray. How is this? Because, dear friends, we are very subject to *fits of worldliness*, if indeed that be not our usual state.

We do not forget to eat; we do not forget to take the shop shutters down; we do not forget to be diligent in business; we do not forget to go to our beds to rest: but we often do forget to wrestle with God in prayer and to spend, as we ought to spend, long periods in consecrated fellowship with our Father and our God.

With too many professors the ledger is so bulky that you cannot move it; and the Bible, representing their devotion, is so small that you might almost put it in your waistcoat pocket. Hours for the world! Moments for Christ!

The world has the best, and our closet the parings of our time. We give our strength and freshness to the ways of mammon and our fatigue and languor to the ways of God. Hence it is that we need to be commanded to attend to that very act which ought to be our greatest happiness, as it is our highest privilege to perform, that is, to meet with our God. 'Call unto me,' saith He, for He knows that we are apt to forget to call upon God. 'What meanest thou, O sleeper? arise, call upon thy God' (Jonah 1:16), is an exhortation which is needed by us as well as by Jonah in the storm.

He understands what *heavy hearts* we have sometimes, when under a sense of sin. Satan says to us, 'Why should you pray? How can you hope to prevail? In vain, thou sayest, I will arise and go to my Father, for thou art not worthy to be one of his hired servants. How canst thou see the king's face after thou has played the traitor against him? How wilt thou dare to approach unto the altar when thou hast thyself defiled it, and when the sacrifice which thou wouldst bring there is a poor, polluted one?'

O brethren, it is well for us that we are commanded to pray, or else in times of heaviness we might give it up. If God command me, unfit as I may be, I will creep to the footstool of grace. And since He says, 'Pray without ceasing,' though my words fail me and my heart itself will wander, yet I will still stammer out the wishes of my hungering soul and say, 'O God, at least teach me to pray and help me to prevail with Thee.'

Are we not commanded to pray also because of our *frequent unbelief?* Unbelief whispers, 'What profit is there if thou shouldst seek the Lord upon such-and-such a matter? Either it is too trivial a matter, or it is too connected with temporals, or else it is a matter in which you have sinned too much, or else it is too high, too hard, to complicated a piece of business. You have no right to take that before God!'

So suggests the foul fiend of Hell. Therefore, there stands written as an everyday precept suitable to every case into which a Christian can be cast, 'Call unto me, call unto me.'

'Art thou sick? Wouldst thou be healed? Cry unto Me, for I am a Great Physician. Does providence trouble thee? Art thou fearful that thou shalt not provide things honest in the sight of man? Call unto Me! Do thy children vex thee? Dost thou feel that which is sharper than an adder's tooth - a

30

thankless child? Call unto Me. Are thy griefs little, yet painful, like small points and pricks of thorns? Call unto Me! Is thy burden heavy as though it would make thy back break beneath its load? Call unto Me!

'Cast thy burden upon the Lord, and he shall sustain thee, he shall never suffer the righteous to be moved.' Ps. 55:22.

We Are Commanded to Pray Both in God's Word and by His Spirit

We must not leave our first part till we have made another remark. We ought to be very glad that God hath given us this commandment in *His Word* that it may be sure and abiding.

It may be a sensible exercise for some of you to find out how often in Scripture you are told to pray. You will be surprised to find how many times such words as these are given:

'Call upon me in the day of trouble: I will deliver thee.' Ps. 50:15.

'Ye people, our out your heart before him.' Ps. 62:8.

'Seek ye the Lord while he may be found, call ye upon him while he is near.' Isa. 55:6.

'Ask, and it shall be given you; seek, and ye shall find; knock, and it shall be opened unto you.' Matt. 7:7.

'Watch ye and pray, lest ye enter into temptation.' Mark 14:38.

'Pray without ceasing.' I Thess. 5:17.

'Let us therefore come boldly unto the throne of grace.' Heb. 4:16.

'Draw nigh to God, and he will draw nigh to you.' James 4:8.

'Continue in prayer.' Col. 4:2.

I need not multiply where I could possibly exhaust. I pick two or three out of this great bag of pearls.

Come, Christian, you ought never to question whether you have a right to pray. You should never ask, 'May I permitted to come into His presence?' When you have so many commands (and God's commands are all promises and all enablings), you may come boldly unto the throne of heavenly grace by the new and living way through the rent veil.

But there are times when God not only commands His people to pray in the Bible, but He also commands them to pray directly *by the motions of His Holy Spirit.*

You who know the inner life comprehend me at once. You feel on a sudden, possibly in the midst of business, the pressing thought that you *must* retire to pray. It may be you do not at first take particular notice of the inclination, but it comes again and again and again - 'Retire and pray!'

I find that in the matter of prayer, I am myself very much like a water wheel which runs well when there is plenty of water, but which turns with very little force when the brook is growing shallow; or, like the ship which flies over the waves, putting out all her canvas when the wind is favourable, but which has to tack about most laboriously when there is but little of the favouring breeze.

32

Now it strikes me that whenever our Lord gives you the special inclination to pray, that you should double your diligence. You ought always to pray and not to faint. Yet when He gives you the special longing after prayer and you feel a peculiar aptness and enjoyment in it, you have, over and above the command which is constantly binding, another command which should compel you to cheerful obedience.

At such times I think we may stand in the position of David, to whom the Lord said, 'When thou hearest the sound of a going in the tops of the mulberry trees, that then thou shalt bestir thyself' (II Sam. 5:24). That going in the tops of the mulberry trees may have been the footfalls of angels hastening to the help of David, and then David was to smite the Philistines and when God's mercies are coming, their footfalls are our desires to pray, and our desires to pray should be at once an indication that the set time to favour Zion is come.

Sow plentifully now, for thou canst sow in hope. Plow joyously now, for thy harvest is sure. Wrestle now, Jacob, for thou art about to be made a prevailing prince, and thy name shall be called Israel., now is thy time, spiritual merchantmen. The market is high, trade much. Thy profit shall be large. See to it that thou usest right well the golden hour, and reap thy harvest whilst the sun shines.

II. AN ANSWER PROMISED

We ought not to tolerate for a minute the ghastly and grievous thought that God will not answer prayer.

God's Nature Demands He Answer Prayer

His nature, as manifested in Christ Jesus, demands it. He

has revealed Himself in the Gospel as a God of love, full of grace and truth; and how can He refuse to help those of His creatures who humbly, in His own appointed way, seek His face and favour?

When the Athenian senate, upon one occasion, found it most convenient to meet together in the open air, as they were sitting in their deliberations , a sparrow, pursued by a hawk, flew in the direction of the senate. Being hard pressed by the bird of prey, it sought shelter in the bosom of one of the senators. He, being a man of rough and vulgar mould, took the bird from his bosom, dashed it on the ground and so killed it. Whereupon the whole senate rose in uproar, and without one single dissenting voice, condemned him to die, as being unworthy of a seat in the senate with them or to be called an Athenian, if he did not render succour to a creature that confided in him.

Can we suppose that the God of Heaven, whose nature is love, could tear out of His bosom the poor fluttering dove that flies from the eagle of justice into the bosom of His mercy? Will He give the invitation to us to seek His face; and when we, as He knows, with so much trepidation of fear, yet summon courage enough to fly into His bosom, will he then be unjust and ungracious enough to forget to hear our cry and to answer us? Let us not think so hardly of the God of Heaven.

God, Giving His Son, Proves His Loved That Will Answer Prayer

Let us recollect next, *His past character* as well as His nature. I mean the character which He has won for Himself by His past deeds of grace.

Consider, my brethren, that one stupendous display of bounty - if I were to mention a thousand I could not give a

better illustration of the character of God than that one deed
- 'He spared not his own Son, but delivered him up for us
all' - and it is not my inference only, but the inspired
conclusion of an apostle - 'how shall he not with him also
freely give us all things?' (Rom. 8:32).

If the Lord did not refuse to listen to my voice when I was
a guilty sinner and an enemy, how can He disregard my cry
now that I am justified and saved! How is it that He heard
the voice of my misery when my heart knew it not and
would not seek relief, if after all he will not hear me now
that I am His child, His friend? The streaming wounds of
Jesus are the sure guarantee for answered prayer.

George Herbert represents in that quaint poem of his,
'The Bag,' the Saviour saying -

> *'If ye have anything to send or write*
> *(I have no bag, but here is room)*
> *Unto My Father's hands and sight,*
> *(Believe Me) it shall safely come.*
> *That I shall mind what you impart*
> *Look, you may put it very near My heart,*
> *Or if hereafter any of friends*
> *Will use Me in this kind, the door*
> *Shall still be open; what he sends*
> *I will present and somewhat more*
> *Not to his hurt.'*

Surely George Herbert's thought was that the atonement
was in itself a guarantee that prayer must be heard, that the
great gash made near the Saviour's heart, which let the light
into the very depths of the heart of Deity, was a proof that
He who sits in Heaven would hear the cry of His people.
You misread Calvary if you think that prayer is useless.

But beloved, we have *the Lord's own promise* for it, and
He is a God that cannot lie. 'Call upon me in the day of

trouble, and I will answer thee.' Has He not said, 'Whatsoever ye shall ask in prayer, believe that ye receive it, and ye shall have it'? We cannot pray, indeed, unless we believe this doctrine; 'for he that cometh to God must believe that he is, and that he is the rewarder of them that diligently seek him'; and if we have any question at all about whether our prayer will be heard, we are comparable to him that wavereth; 'for he who wavereth is like a wave of the sea, driven with the wind and tossed; let not that man think that he shall receive any thing of the Lord.'

Past Experience Shows That God Answers Prayer

Furthermore, it is not necessary, still it may strengthen the point, if we added that *our own experience* leads us to believe that God will answer prayer. I must not speak for you, but I may speak for myself. If there be anything I know, anything that I am quite assured of beyond all question, it is that praying breath is never spent in vain. If no other man here can say it, I dare to say it, and I know that I can prove it.

My own conversion is the result of prayer, long, affectionate, earnest, importunate. Parents prayed for me; God heard their cries, and here I am to preach the Gospel. since then I have adventured upon some things that were far beyond my capacity as I thought; but I have never failed because I have cast myself upon the Lord.

You know as a church that I have scrupled to indulge large ideas of what we might do for God. And we have accomplished all that we purposed. I have sought God's aid, assistance and help in all my manifold undertakings. And though I cannot tell here the story of my private life in God's work, yet if it were written it would be a standing

36

proof that there is a God who answers prayer.

He has heard *my* prayers, not now and then, nor once or twice, but so many times that it has grown into a habit with me to spread my case before God with the absolute certainty that whatsoever I ask of God, He will give to me. It is not now a 'perhaps' or a possibility. I know that my Lord answers me, and I dare not doubt - it were indeed folly if I did.

As I am sure that a certain amount of leverage will lift a weight, so I know that a certain amount of prayer will get anything from God. As the rain cloud brings the shower, so prayer brings the blessing. As spring scatters flowers, so supplication ensures mercies.

In all labour there is profit, but most of all in the work of intercession. I am sure of this, for I have reaped it.

Still remember that prayer is always to be offered in submission to God's will; that when we say God heareth prayer, we do not intend by that, that He always gives us literally what we ask for. We do mean, however, this: He gives us what is best for us; and that if He does not give us the mercy we ask for in silver, He bestows it upon us in gold. If He doth not take away the thorn in the flesh, yet He saith, 'My grace is sufficient for thee,' and that comes to the same in the end.

Lord Bolingbroke said to the Countess of Huntingdon, 'I cannot understand, your ladyship, how you can make out earnest prayer to be consistent with submission to the divine will.'

'My lord,' she said, 'that is a matter of no difficulty. If I were a courtier of some generous king and he gave me permission to ask any favour I pleased of him, I should be sure to put it thus, 'Will your majesty be graciously pleased to grant me such-and-such a favour? But at the same time though I very much desire it, if it would in any way detract from your majesty's honour, of if in your majesty's judgment it should seem better that I did not have this favour, I shall be quite as content to go without it as to receive it. ' So you see I might earnestly offer a petition, and yet I might submissively leave it in the king's hands.'

So with God. We never offer up prayer without inserting that clause, either in spirit or in words, 'Nevertheless, not as I will, but as thou wilt; not my will but thine be done.' We can only pray without an 'if' when we are quite sure that our will must be God's because God's will is fully our will.

III. ENCOURAGEMENT TO FAITH

I come to our third point, which I think is full of encouragement to all those who exercise the hallowed art of prayer: encouragement to faith. 'I will... shew thee great and mighty things, which thou knowest not.'

God Opens Truth in Answer to Prayer

Let us just remark that this was originally spoken to a prophet in prison; therefore, it applies in the first place to *every teacher*; and, indeed, as every teacher must be a learner, it has a bearing upon *every learner* in divine truth. The best way by which a prophet and teacher and learner can know the reserved truths, the higher and more mysterious truths of God, is by waiting upon God in prayer.

I noticed very specially yesterday in reading the Book of the prophet Daniel, how Daniel found out Nebuchadnezzar's dream. The soothsayers, the magicians, the astrologers of the Chaldees brought out their books and their strange-looking instruments, and began to mutter their *abracadabra* and all sorts of mysterious incantations. But they all failed.

What did Daniel do? He set himself to prayer and,

knowing that the prayer of a united body of men has more prevalence than the prayer of one, we find that Daniel called together his brethren and bade them unite with him in earnest prayer that God would be pleased of His infinite mercy to open up the vision.

And in the case of John, who was the Daniel of the New Testament, you remember he saw a book in the right hand of Him who sat on the throne - a book sealed with seven seals which none was found worthy to open or to look thereon.

What did John do? The book was by-and-by opened by the Lion of the tribe of Judah, who had prevailed to open the book; but it is written first before the book was opened, 'I wept much.' Yes, and the tears of John which were his liquid prayers were, as far as he was concerned, the sacred keys by which the folded book was opened.

Brethren in the ministry, you who are teachers in the Sunday school, and all of you who are learners in the college of Christ Jesus, I pray you remember that prayer is your best means of study. Like Daniel, you shall understand the dream and the interpretation thereof, when you have sought unto God; and, like John, you shall see the seven seals of precious truth unloosed, after that you have wept much.

'Yea, if thou criest after knowledge, and liftest up thy voice for understanding; If thou seekest her as silver, and searchest for her as for hid treasures; Then shalt thou understand the fear of the Lord, and find the knowledge of God.' Prov. 2:3-5.

Stones are not broken except by an earnest use of the hammer; and the stone-breaker usually goes down on his knees. Use the hammer of vengeance and let the knee of prayer be exercised, too; and there is not a stony doctrine in

Revelation which is useful for you to understand, which will not fly into shivers under the exercise of prayer and faith.

'Bene orasse est bene studuisse' was a wise sentence of Luther, which has been so often quoted, that we hardly venture but to hint at it. 'To have prayed well is to have studied well.'

You may force your way through anything with the leverage of prayers. Thoughts and reasonings may be like the steel wedges which may open a way into truth; but prayer is the lever, the prise which forces open the iron chest of sacred mystery, that we may get the treasure that is hidden therein for those who can force their way to reach it.

The kingdom of Heaven still suffereth violence, and the violent taketh it by force. Take care that ye work away with the mighty implement of prayer, and nothing can stand against you.

Blessed Experience and Fellowship With God in Answer to Prayer

We must not, however, stop there. We have applied the text to only once case; it is applicable to a hundred. We single out another. The *saint may expect to discover deeper experience* and to know more of the higher spiritual life, by being much in prayer. There are different translations of my text. One version renders it, 'I will shew thee great and fortified things which thou knowest not.' Another reads it, 'Great and reserved things which thou knowest not.'

Now, all the developments of spiritual life are not alike easy of attainment. There are common frames and feelings of repentance and faith and joy and hope which are enjoyed by the entire family; but there is an upper realm of rapture, of communion and conscious union with Christ which is far from being the common dwelling place of believers.

All believers see Christ, but all believers do not put their fingers into the prints of the nails nor thrust their hand into His side. We have not all the high privilege of John to lean upon Jesus' bosom, nor of Paul, to be caught up into the third Heaven.

In the ark of salvation we find a lower, second and third story. All are in the ark, but all are not in the same story. Most Christians, as to the river of experience, are only up to the ankles; some others have waded till the stream is up to the knees; a few find it breast-high; and but a few - oh! how few! - find it a river to swim in, the bottom of which they cannot touch.

My brethren, there are heights in experimental knowledge of the things of God which the eagle's eye of acumen and philosophic thought have never seen; and there are secret paths which the lion's whelp of reason and judgment hath not as yet learned to travel. God alone can bear us there, but the chariot in which He takes us up and the fiery steeds with which that chariot is dragged are prevailing prayers.

Prevailing prayer is victorious over the God of mercy.

'Yea, he had power over the angel, and prevailed: he wept, and made supplication unto him: he found him in Bethel, and there he spake with us.' Hosea 12:4.

Prevailing prayer takes the Christian to Carmel and enables him to cover Heaven with clouds of blessing and earth with floods of mercy. Prevailing prayer bears the Christian aloft to Pisgah and shows him the inheritance reserved; ay, and it elevates him to Tabor and transfigures him, till in the likeness of his Lord, as He is, so are we also in this world.

If you would reach to something higher than ordinary grovelling experience, look to the Rock that is higher than you, and look with the eye of faith through the windows of importunate prayer.

To grow in experience, then, there must be much prayer.

Here is Comfort for Those Who Are Sorely Tired

You must have patience with me while I apply this text to two or three more cases. It is certainly true of *sufferer under trial*. If he waits upon God in prayer much, he shall receive greater deliverances than he has ever dreamed of - 'great and mighty things, which thou knowest not.'

Here is Jeremiah's testimony: 'Thou drewest near in the day that I called upon thee; thou saidst, Fear not. O Lord, thou hast pleaded the causes of my soul; thou hast redeemed my life' (Lam. 3:57,58).

And David's is the same: 'I called upon the Lord in distress: the Lord answered me, and set me in a large place' (Ps. 118:5). 'I will praise thee: for thou hast heard me, and art become my salvation' (vs.21).

Yet again: 'Then they cried unto the Lord in their trouble, and he delivered them out of their distresses. And he led them forth by the right way, that they might go to a city of habitation.' (Ps. 107:7).

'My husband is dead,' said the poor woman, 'and my creditor is come to take my two sons as bondsmen.' She hoped Elijah would possibly say, 'What are your debts? I will pay them.' Instead of that he multiples her oil till it is written, 'Go thou and pay thy debts, and' - what was the 'and'? - 'live thou and thy children upon the rest.' So often it will happen that God will not only help His people through the miry places of the way, so that they may just stand on the other side of the slough, but He will bring them safely far on the journey.

That was a remarkable miracle, when in the midst of the storm, Jesus Christ came walking upon the sea, the disciples received Him into the ship, and not only was the sea calm, but it is recorded, 'Immediately the ship was at the land whither they went.' That was a mercy over and above what they asked. I sometimes hear you pray and make use of a quotation which is not in the Bible. I do not know what we can ask or what we can think. But it is said, 'He is able to do exceeding abundantly above what we ask or even think.' Let us, then, dear friends, when we are in great trial, only say, 'Now I am in prison like Jeremiah; I will pray as he did, for I have God's command to do it; and I will look out as he did, expecting that He will show me reserved mercies which I know nothing of at present.'

He will not merely bring His people through the battle, covering their heads in it, but He will bring them forth with banners waving, to divide the spoil with the mighty, and to claim their portion with the strong.

Expect great things of a God who gives such great promises.

Encouragement for Christian Workers

Again, here is *encouragement for the worker*. My dear friends, wait upon God much in prayer, and you have the promise that He will do greater things for you than you know of. We know not how much capacity for usefulness there may be in us. That ass's jawbone lying there upon the earth, what can it do? Nobody knows what it can do. It gets into Samson's hands, what can it *not* do? No one knows what it cannot do now that a Samson wields it.

And you, friend, have often thought yourself to be as contemptible as that bone, and you have said, 'What can I

43

do?' Ay, but when Christ by His Spirit grips you, what can you not do? Truly you may adopt Paul's language and say, 'I can do all things through Christ which strengtheneth me' (Phil. 4:13).

However, do not depend upon prayer without effort.

In a certain school there was one girl who knew the Lord, a very gracious, simple-hearted, trustful child. As usual, grace developed itself in the child according to the child's position. Her lessons were always best said of any in the class.

Another girl said to her, 'How is it that your lessons are always so well said?'

'I pray God to help me,' she said, 'to learn my lesson.'

Thought the other, *Well, then, I will do the same.*

The next morning when she stood up in the class, she knew nothing; and when she was in disgrace she complained to the other, 'Why, I prayed God to help me learn my lesson, and I do not know anything of it. What is the use of prayer?'

'But did you sit down and try to learn it?'

'Oh, no,' she said, 'I never looked at the book.'

'Ah,' then said the other, 'I asked God to help me to learn my lesson; but I then sat down to it studiously, and I kept at it till I new it well, and I learned it easily because my earnest desire, which I had expressed to God, was, 'Help me to be diligent in endeavouring to do my duty.'

So it is with some who come up to prayer meetings and pray then they fold their arms and go away hoping that God's work will go on. Like the Negro woman singing, 'Fly abroad, thou mighty Gospel,' but not putting a penny in the plate; so that her friend touched her and said, 'But how can it fly if you don't give it wings to fly with?'

There be many who appear to be very mighty in prayer, wondrous in supplications; but then they require God to do what they can do themselves; and, therefore, God does nothing at all for them. 'I shall leave my camel untied,' said an Arab once to Mahomet, 'and trust to providence.' 'Tie it up tight,' said Mahomet, 'and then trust to providence.'

So you who say, 'I shall pray and trust my church, or my class, or my work to God's goodness,' may rather hear the voice of experience and wisdom which says, 'Do thy best; work as if all rested upon thy toil; as if thy own arm would bring thy salvation'; 'and when thou hast done all, cast thyself on Him without whom it is in vain to rise up early and to sit up late, and to eat the bread of carefulness; and if He speed thee, give Him the praise.'

Here Is Comfort for Intercessors

I shall not detain you many minutes longer, but I want you to notice that this promise ought to prove useful for the comforting of those who are intercessors for others. You who are calling upon God to save your children, to bless your neighbours, to remember your husbands or your wives in mercy, may take comfort from this, 'I will ... shew thee great and mighty things, which thou knowest not.'

A celebrated minister in the last century, one Mr. Bailey, was the child of a godly mother. This mother had almost ceased to pray for her husband, who was a man of a most ungodly stamp and a bitter persecutor. The mother prayed for her boy; and while he was yet eleven or twelve years of age, eternal mercy met with him. So sweetly instructed was the child in the things of the kingdom of God that the mother requested him - and for some time he always did so - to conduct family prayer in the house.

Morning and evening this little one laid open the Bible; and though the father would not deign to stop for the family prayer, yet on one occasion he was rather curious to know 'what sort of an out the boy would make of it,' so he stopped on the other side of the door. God blessed the prayer of his

45

own child under thirteen years of age to his conversion.

The mother might well have read my text with streaming eyes, and said, 'Yes, Lord, Thou hast shown me great and mighty things which I knew not. Thou hast not only saved my boy, but through my boy Thou hast brought my husband to the truth.'

You cannot guess how greatly God will bless you. Only go and stand at His door - you cannot tell what is in reserve for you. If you do not beg at all, you will get nothing; but if you beg, He may not only give you, as it were, the bones and broken meat, but He may say to the servant at His table, 'Take thou that dainty meat and set that before the poor man.'

Ruth went to glean; she expected to get a few good ears. But Boaz said, 'Let her glean even among the sheaves, and rebuke her not.' He said moreover to her, 'At mealtime come thou hither, and eat of the bread, and dip thy morsel in the vinegar.' Nay, she found a husband where she only expected to find a handful of barley.

So in prayer for others, God may give us such mercies that we shall be astounded at them, since we expected but little. Hear what is said of Job and learn its lesson:

'And ... the Lord said ... my servant Job shall pray for you: for him will I accept; lest I deal with you after your folly, in that ye have not spoken of me the thing which is right, like my servant Job ... And the Lord turned the captivity of Job, when he prayed for his friends: also the Lord gave Job twice as much as he had before.' Job 42:7,8,10.

Now, this word to close with. Some of you are seekers for your own conversion. God has quickened you to solemn prayer about your own souls. You are not content to go to Hell. You want Heaven. You want washing in the precious blood. You want eternal life. Dear friends, I pray take you this text - God Himself speaks it to you - 'Call unto me, and I will answer thee, and shew thee great and mighty things, which thou knowest not.' At once take God at His word. Get home, go into you chamber, shut the door and try Him.

Young man, I say, try the Lord. Young woman, prove Him, see whether He be true or not. If God be true, you cannot seek mercy at His hands through Jesus Christ and get a negative reply. He must, for His own promise and character, bind Him to it, open mercy's gate to you who knock with all your hearts.

God help you, believing in Christ Jesus, to cry aloud unto God, and His answer of peace is already on the way to meet you. You shall hear Him say, 'Your sins which are many are all forgiven.'

The Lord bless you for His love's sake. Amen.

3

God Answers Prayer

BILLY SUNDAY

Jesus Christ the same yesterday, and to day, and for ever ...' Heb. 13:8.

We live in a very practical age. People do things, not because the law compels them, but because they get something for their efforts.

The Motto of today seems to be: Where do I come in on this? What do I get out of it?

We are willing to invest our money if we get good returns. That's right. We gladly try the doctor's treatment. We are a nation of tasters. Is the game worth the candle?

We do not have to comprehend the process in order to enjoy its results.

I do not understand electricity; but turn the switch, and the room is flooded with light.

I do not understand the mechanism of the telephone; but I call the number, and I get my friends on the wire.

I do not understand the process of digestion, but I eat.

I do not understand the anatomy of the body, but I take the

doctor's medicine.

I pray because of its proved helpfulness, but I cannot understand its mysteries.

If I never used an elevator until I understood how it worked, I would stay downstairs all my life.

If I never used an automobile until I understood its mechanism, I would have to walk.

If I never looked at my watch until I could make one, I would never know the time of day.

So if I never prayed until I understood all its mysteries, I would be a stranger to God all my days.

Nobody knows what takes place when we drop a lump of sugar in the coffee, whether the change is mechanical or chemical. All we know is that the sugar sweetens the coffee, and that's all we need to know.

There has never been a great moral or spiritual awakening in history that did not root itself in prayer. At Pentecost, where the Holy Spirit came down and where the church was born, they held a ten-day prayer meeting.

A prominent man told me he had visited scores of churches; yet he could not gather from what was preached whether the preacher was a follower of Confucius, Mohammed, Zoroaster, or Christ.

No wonder crime is rampant when they make individual opinion, instead of the Bible, the seat of authority. Rebellion is bound to follow.

No wonder that under this tidal wave of materialism, our churches have lost hundreds of thousands of members. They are trying to divert attention from their failure by attacking evangelism - the one force and power that has kept the spiritual flame alive.

Prayer is beginning to be looked upon as old-fashioned. People are not praying today. We are facing one of the greatest crises in our history. The one thing that will save our nation is a sweeping revival of religion.

Blackstone said that in his day you could not tell from what the preachers said whether they were heathen or Christian. Yet out of all this darkness came the revival under Wesley and Whitefield, which gave birth to the Methodist church with nine million adherents.

GOD ANSWERS PRAYER

Phillips Brooks said that prayer is not overcoming God's reluctance, but a laying hold of His willingness.

Abraham prayed for a son, and God gave him a posterity like the sands of the sea. He prayed for Ishmael; God spared the boy's life and made of him a great nation. He prayed for Sodom. God heard his prayer and postponed the day of doom.

Jacob prayed for a favourable reception by Esau.
Moses prayed for the forgiveness of the people.
Gideon prayed God to overthrow the Midianites.
Elijah prayed, and God heard and answered by fire.
Joshua prayed, and Achan was discovered.
Hannah prayed, and Samuel was born.
Hezekiah prayed, and 185,000 Assyrians died.
Daniel prayed, and the lions were muzzled.

The apostles prayed, and the Holy Spirit came down.
Not one of these would have happened without prayer.

Luther prayed, and the Reformation was the result.
Knox prayed, and Scotland trembled.
Brainerd prayed, and the Indians were subdued.
Wesley prayed, and millions were moved Godward.
Whitefield prayed, and thousands were converted.
Finney prayed, and mighty revivals resulted.

Taylor prayed, and the great China Inland Mission was born.

Mueller prayed, and more than seven million dollars were sent in to feed thousands of orphans.

Auntie Cook prayed; Moody was anointed, and the Moody Bible Institute was launched.

Men are always praying; God is always answering.

God has to make some of us wait on the side track while His through-trains rush by.

A plain seaman stood on watch on a US battleship hundreds of miles out to sea on the Atlantic. A wireless message was handed to him, reading, 'Little Donald died yesterday. Funeral Wednesday. Can you come?' It was signed 'Mary.' He forgot his duty and saw only the smiling face of his baby he had left three months before. He burst into tears. The captain asked, 'What's the matter?' He handed the officer the message.

'Where do you live?' asked the captain.

'Cleveland, Ohio, Sir,' replied the seamen.

The captain barked some orders to the engine room and then sent out a wireless message. It wasn't long before a cruiser was sighted; the sailor was put upon her, and she raced toward New York.

Another wireless, and a fast torpedo boat came over the horizon. He was lowered on to her. She made all speed to New York harbour, where the sailor was put in a cab and driven hurriedly to the Pennsylvanian depot. He rushed up to the ticket office to inquire when the next train left for Cleveland. The agent told him it would leave in three minutes. He tore down the stairs and climbed aboard just as the train was pulling out of the station. He reached his home and Mary's arms just as the minister arose to deliver his sermon.

All the power of the United States Navy was placed at his disposal.

GOD ANSWERS PRAYER THROUGH HUMAN COOPERATION

We need more prayer sense. It takes considerable planning before we get ready to pray, 'O Lord, I want a house.' Then say, 'Amen' with a hammer and saw. Or, 'O Lord, I want to be a strong Christian.' Then say 'Amen' on your knees, with a membership in a church; otherwise your prayers will not great much commotion in Heaven.

We pray, 'O Lord, save the world.' That's an easy and cheap way. If we are in earnest we'll say 'Amen' with our hands, our hearts, our money, and really get down on our knees and actually down to business.

Bishop Whipple was the Episcopal bishop of Minnesota. He tells of an Episcopal clergyman who was called to comfort a dying girl. The house in which she lay was kept by in incarnate fiend, who was offended that the clergyman should come to the home to pray. The woman met him with a butcher knife in hand and told him he could not pray in her house.

The clergyman had a cane. He said, 'Madame, I came down here to commend this dying girl to Jesus. I want you to know that I can pray just as well with my eyes open as shut. If you stir one step while I pray, I will crack your head with this stick.' The woman never budged. I like a fellow like that, don't you?

Too many Christians are slovenly in prayer. They are careless and thoughtless; they almost yawn in God's presence; they do not concentrate their thoughts.

'How' is one of the biggest words in our language. We are all curious. We are not satisfied to see a thing done, but we ask, 'How?' That's why a child likes to take a watch apart.

Too many of us, when we take our problems to the Lord, drop our prayers before His throne and seem to say, 'I wash my hands. Now it's up to You.'

We must live and act in such a way that God can answer our prayers. Some think and teach that God has a mysterious wand to wave over the sick while the patient refuses to cooperate. If a man prays for health, he must use every means to keep himself well.

Moody was asked to pray for the recovery of a sick preacher. 'No, I won't,' he said. 'He does ten day's work in five and eats everything in sight.'

If a man prays for the ability to win souls, he will naturally do personal work.

If a man prays for a job, he will read the want ads.

If he prays for a wife, he will go out and meet women socially and not wait for some woman to come and say, 'Good morning. I'm your wife. The Lord sent me to you.'

Some try to make prayer a substitute for work. Real prayer is teamwork with the Lord. It's God at the front end leading us on. He wants us to be at the back end following.

Get rid of the idea that prayer is one-power affair where God is the conductor and motorman.

A man was out in a boat with a black man. A storm arose. The man became frightened and said, 'Moses, shall we pray or row?'

The black man replied, 'Boss, let's mix'em. Pray and row.'

Dr. Norman McLeod was a big burly fellow. His friend was small. The latter said, 'Dr. McLeod, let's pray.' The Highland boatman said, 'Na, na, Mon! Let the wee mon pray, and the big mon take an oar.'

In all human history certain crises have arisen when the help of man was vain.

Dr. Jessup and Dr. Bliss of Syria sat together in Constantinople, both in tears of the edict of the Sultan ordering all American schools closed. Finally Dr. Bliss said, 'Let's lay this before the Sultan of Heaven.' They prayed all night. The next day the Sultan died and the edict was recalled.

Moody said that Jesus never taught His disciples how to preach, but how to pray; not how to run a church, or how to raise money, but how to pray.

Beecher said, 'I pray on the principle that wine knocks the cork out of the bottle. Where there is inward fermentation there must be a vent.'

WE DO NOT PUT ENOUGH TRUST IN PRAYER

Henry Drummond tells of a little girl who was crossing the ocean. She dropped her doll overboard and, running to the captain, asked him to stop the ship and pick up her dolly. She had seen him do that to rescue a man, and she thought he was cruel when he refused. When the ship reached port, the captain bought her the finest doll he could find. He had refused her request, but he gave her something much better.

A little girl went to a hospital for an operation. The doctor said, 'I must put you to sleep, and when you wake up you'll be better.' She replied, 'Oh, before I go to sleep, I always pray.' She jumped down and prayed, 'Now I lay me down to sleep.' The doctors and nurses bowed their heads and waited. I believe that doctor received divine help in that special case.

During the first World's Fair in Chicago in 1893, Mr. Moody carried on numberless evangelistic meetings. He secured many speakers from abroad, rented halls and engaged theatres. It took a great deal of money to carry on such extensive work.

One day Mr. Moody invited a dozen men to luncheon at a downtown hotel. He said to them, 'I didn't invite you here merely to eat. I invited you because I believe you have power in prayer. I need seven thousand dollars to keep this work going.'

Before luncheon was served, they all definitely prayed for seven thousand dollars. Before lunch was finished, Moody was handed a telegram which read:

We, your friends at Northfield, became impressed that you must have money to carry on your work in Chicago. We have taken an offering amounting to seven thousand dollars. I am mailing you a draft for that amount, praying God's richest blessings upon you and His cause.

The prayers reached God, and He sent the answer via Northfield.

Charles M. Alexander went into a bank in England to see one of its officers. While waiting, he picked up a blotter and wrote on it, 'Pray through.' The officer was detained. and Mr. Alexander kept on writing until he had covered the blotter with the words, 'Pray through.'

After he left the room, a businessman was ushered into the same room to wait. He was discouraged and troubled. Picking up the blotter, he read it over and over again, and suddenly exclaimed, 'Why that's just the message I need. I've tried to worry it through; now I'll pray it through.'

Don't stop praying; the Lord is nigh.
Don't stop praying; He'll hear your cry.
God has promised; He is true!
Don't stop praying; He'll answer you.

4

Prayers of the Bible

D. L. MOODY

Those who have left the deepest impression on this sin-cursed earth have been men and women of prayer. You will find that prayer has been the mighty power that has moved not only God, but man.

ABRAHAM

Abraham was a man of prayer, and angels came down from Heaven to converse with him.

JACOB

Jacob's prayer was answered in the wonderful interview at Peniel that resulted in having such a mighty blessing and in softening the heart of his brother Esau.

HANNAH

The child Samuel was given in answer to Hannah's prayer.

ELIJAH

Elijah's prayer closed up the heavens for three years and six months, and he prayed again and the heavens gave rain.

The Apostle James tells us that the Prophet Elijah was a man 'subject to like passions as we are.' I am thankful that those men and women who were so mighty in prayer were just like ourselves. We are apt to think that those prophets and mighty men and women of old time were different from what we are. To be sure, they lived in a much darker age, but they were of like passions with ourselves.

WONDERFUL BIBLE EXAMPLES OF PRAYERS ANSWERED

We read on that other occasion Elijah brought down fire on Mount Carmel. The prophets of Baal cried long and loud, but no answer came. The God of Elijah heard and answered his prayer.

Let us remember that the God of Elijah still lives. The prophet was translated and went up to Heaven, but his God still lives, and we have the same access to Him that Elijah had. We have the same warrant to go to God and ask the fire from Heaven to come down and consume our lusts and passions - to burn up our dross, and let Christ shine through us.

ELISHA

Elisha prayed, and life came back to a dead child. Many of our children are dead in trespasses and sins. Let us do as Elisha did. Let us entreat God to raise them up in answer to our prayers.

MANASSEH

Manasseh the king was a wicked man who had done everything he could against the God of his father; yet in Babylon, when he cried to God, his cry was heard, and he was taken out of prison and put on the throne at Jerusalem. Surely if God gave heed to the prayer of wicked Manasseh, He will hear ours in the time of our distress.

Is not his a time of distress with a great number of our fellow men? Are there not many among us whose hearts are burdened? As we go to the throne of grace, let us remember that God answers prayer.

SAMSON

Look again at Samson. He prayed, and his strength came back so that he slew more at his death than during his life. He was a restored backslider, and he had power with God. If those who have been backsliders will but return to God, they will see how quickly God will answer prayer.

JOB

Job prayed, and his captivity was turned. Light came in the place of darkness, and God lifted him up above the height of his former prosperity - in answer to prayer.

DANIEL

Daniel prayed to God, and Gabriel came to tell him that he was a man greatly beloved of God. Three times that message came to him from Heaven in answer to prayer. The secrets of Heaven were imparted to him, and he was told that God's Son was going to be cut off for the sins of His people.

CORNELIUS

We find also that Cornelius prayed. And Peter was sent to tell him words whereby he and his should be saved. In answer to prayer, this great blessing came upon him and his household. Peter had gone up to the housetop to pray in the afternoon when he had that wonderful vision of the sheet let down from Heaven. It was when prayer was made without ceasing unto God for Peter that the angel was sent to deliver him.

So all through the Scriptures you will find that, when believing prayer went up to God, the answer came down. I think it would be a very interesting study to go right through the Bible and see what has happened while God's people have been on their knees calling upon Him. Certainly the study would greatly strengthen our faith - showing, as it would, how wonderfully God has heard and delivered when the cry has gone up to Him for help.

PAUL AND SILAS

Look at Paul and Silas in the prison at Philippi. As they prayed and sang praises, the place was shaken, and the jailor was converted. Probably that one conversion has done more than any other recorded in the Bible to bring people into the Kingdom of God. How many have been blessed in seeking to answer the question - 'What must I do to be saved?' It was the prayer of these two godly men that brought the jailor to his knees and that brought blessing to him and his family.

STEPHEN

You remember how, as Stephen prayed and looked up, he saw the heavens opened and the Son of man at the right hand of God. The light of Heaven fell on his face so that it shone. Remember, too, how the face of Moses shone as he came down from the Mount; he had been in communion with God.

So when we get really into communion with God, He lifts up His countenance upon us. And instead of our having gloomy looks, our faces will shine because God has heard and answered our prayers.

JESUS, A MAN OF PRAYER

I want to call special attention to Christ as an example for us in all things; in nothing more than in prayer. We read that Christ prayed to His Father for everything. Every great crisis in His life was preceded by prayer. Let me quote a few passages.

I never noticed till a few years ago that Christ was praying at His baptism. As He prayed, the heavens were opened, and the Holy Ghost descended on Him. Another great event in His life was His Transfiguration. 'As he prayed, the fashion of his countenance was altered, and his raiment was white and glistening.'

We read again, ' It came to pass in those days that he went out into a mountain to pray, and continued all night in prayer to God.' This is the only place where it is recorded that the Saviour spent a whole night in prayer.

What was about to take place? When He came down from the mountain, He gathered His disciples around Him and preached that great discourse known as the Sermon on the Mount - the most wonderful sermon that has ever been preached to mortal men. Probably no sermon has done so much good, and it was preceded by a night of prayer. If our sermons are going to reach the hearts and consciences of the people, we must be much in prayer to God that there may be power with the Word.

In the Gospel of John we read that Jesus at the grave of Lazarus lifted up His eyes to Heaven and said, 'Father, I thank thee that thou hast heard me; and I knew that thou hearest me always; but because of the people which stand by I said it, that they may believe that thou hast sent me.'

Notice that before He spoke the dead to life, He spoke to His Father. If our spiritually dead ones are to be raised, we must first get power with God. The reason we so often fail in moving our fellow men is that we try to win them without first getting power with God. Jesus was in communion with His Father, and so He could be assured that His prayers were heard.

We read again, in the 12th of John, that He prayed to the Father. I think this is one of the saddest chapters in the whole Bible. He was about to leave the Jewish nation and to make atonement for the sin of the world. Hear what He says: 'Now is my soul troubled, and what shall I say? Father, save me from this hour; but for this cause came I unto this hour.'

THE SHADOW OF THE CROSS

He was almost under the shadow of the cross. The

iniquities of mankind were about to be laid upon Him. One of His twelve disciples was going to deny Him and swear he never knew Him. Another was to sell Him for thirty pieces of silver. All were to forsake Him and flee. His soul was exceeding sorrowful, and He prays. When His soul was troubles, God spoke to Him. Then in the Garden of Gethsemane, while He prayed, an angel appeared to strengthen Him. In answer to His cry, 'Father, glorify thy name,' He hears a voice coming down from the glory - 'I have glorified it, and will glorify it again.'

Another memorable prayer of our Lord was in the Garden of Gethsemane: 'He was withdrawn from them about a stone's cast, and kneeled down and prayed.'

I would draw your attention to the recorded fact that four times the answer came right down from Heaven while the Saviour prayed to God. The first time was at His baptism, when the heavens were opened, and the Spirit descended upon Him in answer to His prayer. Again, on the Mount of Transfiguration God appeared and spoke to Him. Then when the Greeks came desiring to see Him, the voice of God was heard responding to His call. And again, when He cried to the Father in midst of His agony, a direct response was given. These things are recorded, I doubt not, that we may be encouraged to pray.

We read that His disciples came to Him and said, 'Lord, teach us to pray.' It is not recorded that He taught them how to preach. I have often said that I would rather know how to pray like Daniel than to preach like Gabriel. If you get love into your soul so that the grace of God may come down in answer to prayer, there will be no trouble about reaching the people. It is not by eloquent sermons that perishing souls are going to be reached. We need the power of God in order that the blessing may come down.

The prayer our Lord taught His disciples is commonly called the Lord's Prayer. I think that the Lord's Prayer, more properly, is that in the 17th of John. That is the longest prayer on record that Jesus made. You can read it slowly and carefully in about four of five minutes.

SHORT PRAYERS IN PUBLIC

I think we may learn a lesson here. Our Master's prayers were short when offered in public. When He was alone with God, that was a different thing. And He could spend the whole night in communion with His Father.

My experience is that those who pray most in their closets generally make short prayers in public. Long prayers are too often not prayers at all, and they weary the people.

How short the publican's prayer was: 'God be merciful to me a sinner!' The Syrophenician woman's was shorter still: 'Lord, help me!' She went right to the mark, and she got what she wanted. The prayer of the thief on the cross was a short one: 'Lord, remember me when thou comest into thy kingdom!' Peter's prayer was, 'Lord, save me!'

So if you go through the Scriptures, you will find that He made seven requests - one for Himself, four for His disciples around Him, and two for the disciples of succeeding ages. Six times in that one prayer He repeats that God had sent Him. The world looked upon Him as an impostor; and He wanted them to know that He was Heaven-sent. He speaks of the world nine times and makes mention of His disciples and those who believe on Him fifty times.

Christ's last prayer on the cross was a short one: 'Father, forgive them, for they know not what they do.' I believe that prayer was answered. We find that right there in front of the cross, a Roman centurion was converted. It was probably in answer to the Saviour's prayer. The conversion of the thief, I believe, was in answer to that prayer of our blessed Lord. Saul of Tarsus may have heard it, and the words may have followed him as he travelled to Damascus; so that when the

Lord spoke to him on the way, he may have recognised the voice. One thing we do know - that on the day of Pentecost some of the enemies of the Lord were converted. Surely that was in answer to the prayer, 'Father, forgive them!'

MEN OF GOD ARE MEN OF PRAYER

Hence we see that prayer holds a high place among the exercises of a spiritual life. All God's people have been praying people.

BAXTER
Look, for instance, at Baxter! He stained his study walls with praying breath. And after he was anointed with the unction of the Holy Ghost, sent a river of living water over Kidderminster, and converted hundreds.

LUTHER
Luther and his companions were men of such mighty pleading with God that they broke the spell of ages and laid nations subdued at the foot of the cross.

KNOX
John Knox grasped all Scotland in his strong arms of faith. His prayers terrified tyrants.

WHITEFIELD
Whitefield, after much holy, faithful closet-pleading, went to the Devil's fair and took more than a thousand souls out of the paw of the lion in one day.

WESLEY
See a praying Wesley turn more than ten thousand souls to the Lord!

FINNEY
Look at the praying Finney, whose prayers, faith, sermons and writings have shaken this whole country and sent a wave of blessing through the churches on both sides of the sea.

Dr. Guthrie thus speaks of prayer and its necessity:

'The first true sign of spiritual life, prayer, is also the means of maintaining it. Man can as well live physically without breathing, as spiritually without praying. There is a class of animals - the cetaceous, neither fish nor sea-fowl - that inhabits the deep. It is their home. They never leave it for the shore. Yet, though swimming beneath its waves and sounding its darkest depths, they have ever and anon to rise to the surface that they may breathe the air. Without that, these monarchs of the deep could not exist in the dense element in which they live, and move, and have their being.

And some like what is imposed on them by a physical necessity, the Christian has to do by a spiritual one. It is by ever and anon ascending up to God, by rising through prayer into a loftier, purer region for supplies of Divine grave, that he maintains his spiritual life.

Prevent these animals from rising to the surface, and they die for want of breath. Prevent the Christian from rising to God, and he dies for want of prayer. 'Give me children,' cried Rachel, 'or else I die.' 'Let me breathe,' says a man gasping, 'or else I die.' 'Let me pray,' says the Christian, 'or else I die.''

'Since I began,' said Dr. Payson, when a student, 'to beg God's blessing on my studies, I have done more in one week than in the whole year before.'

Luther, when most pressed with work, said, 'I have so much to do that I cannot get on without three hours a day praying.'

And not only do theologians think and speak highly of prayer; men of all ranks and positions in life have felt the same.

General Havelock rose at four o'clock, if the hour for marching was six, rather than lose the precious privilege of communion with God before setting out.

Sir Matthew Hale says, 'If I omit praying and reading God's Word in the morning, nothing goes well all day.'

'A great part of my time,' said M'Cheyne, 'is spent in getting my heart in tune for prayer. It is the link that connects earth with Heaven.'

A comprehensive view of the subject will show that there are nine elements which are essential to true prayer.

The first is adoration. We cannot meet God on a level at the start. We much approach Him as One far beyond our reach or sight.

The next is confession. Sin must be put out of the way. We cannot have any communion with God while there is any transgression between us. If there stands some wrong you have done a man, you cannot expect that man's favour until you go to him and confess the fault.

Restitution is another. We have to make good the wrong, wherever possible.

Thanksgiving is the next. We must be thankful for what God has done for us already.

Then comes forgiveness, and then unity. And then for prayer, such as these things produce, there must be faith.

Thus influenced, we shall be ready to offer direct petition. We hear a good deal of praying that is just exhorting, and if you did not see the man's eyes closed, you would suppose he were preaching. Then, much that is called prayer is simply finding fault. There needs to be more *petition* in our prayers.

After all these, there must come submission. While praying, we must be ready to accept the will of God.

5

Prayer And The Promise

E. M. BOUNDS

Without the promise prayer is eccentric and baseless. Without prayer, the promise is dim, voiceless, shadowy, and impersonal. The promise makes prayer dauntless and irresistible. The Apostle Peter declares that God has given to us 'exceeding great and precious promises.' 'Precious' and 'exceeding great' promises they are, and for this very cause we are to 'add to our faith,' and supply virtue. It is the addition which makes the promises current and beneficial to us. It is prayer which makes the promises weighty, precious and practical. The Apostle Paul did not hesitate to declare that God's grace so richly promised was made operative and efficient by prayer. 'Ye also helping together by prayer for us.'

The promises of God are 'exceeding great and precious,' words which clearly indicate their great value and their broad reach, as grounds upon which to base our expectations in praying. howsoever exceeding great and precious they are, their realisation, the possibility and condition of that realisation, are based on prayer. how glorious are these promises to the believing saints and to the whole Church! How the brightness and bloom, the fruitage and cloudless midday glory of the future beam on us through the promises of God! Yet these promises never brought hope to bloom or fruit to a prayerless heart. Neither could these promises, were they a thousandfold increased in number and preciousness, bring millennium glory to a prayerless Church. Prayer makes the promise rich, fruitful and a conscious reality.

Prayer as a spiritual energy, and illustrated in its enlarged and mighty working, makes way for and brings into practical realisation the promises of God.

PROMISES FOR THE PRESENT AND THE FUTURE

God's promises cover all things which pertain to life and godliness, which relate to body and soul, which have to do with time and eternity. These promises bless the present and stretch out in their benefactions to the illimitable and eternal future. Prayer holds these promises in keeping and in fruition. Promises are God's golden fruit to be plucked by the hand of prayer. Promises are God's incorruptible seed, to be sown and tilled by prayer.

Prayer and the promises are interdependent. The promise inspires and energises prayer, but prayer locates the promise, and gives it realisation and location. The promise is like the blessed rain falling in full showers, but prayer, like the pipes, which transmit, preserve and direct the rain, localises and precipitates these promises, until they become local and personal, and bless, refresh, and fertilise. Prayer takes hold of the promise and conducts it to its marvellous ends, removes the obstacles, and makes a highway for the promise to its glorious fulfilment.

SOME EXAMPLES

While God's promises are 'exceeding great and precious,' they are specific, clear and personal. How pointed and plain God's promise to Abraham:

'And the angel of the Lord called unto Abraham out of heaven the second time,

'And said, By myself have I sworn, saith the Lord, for because thou hast done this thing, and hast not withheld thy son, thine only son;

'That in blessing I will bless thee, and in multiplying I will multiply thy seed as the stars of heaven, and as the sand which is upon the seashore; and thy seed shall possess the gate of his enemies;

'And in thy seed shall all the nations of the earth be blessed; because thou hast obeyed my voice.'

But Rebekah through whom the promise is to flow is childless. her barren womb forms an invincible obstacle to the fulfilment of God's promise. But in the course of time children are born to her.

Isaac becomes a man of prayer through whom the promise is to be realised, and so we read:

'And Isaac entreated the Lord for his wife, because she was barren, and the Lord was entreated for him, and Rebekah his wife conceived.'

Isaac's praying opened the way for the fulfilment of God's promise, and carried it on to its marvellous fulfilment, and made the promise effectual in bringing forth marvellous results.

God spoke to Jacob and made definite promises to him:

'Return unto the land of thy fathers, and to thy kindred, and I will be with thee.'

Jacob promptly moves out on the promise, but Esau confronts him with his awakened vengeance and his murderous intention, more dreadful because of the long years, unappeased and waiting. Jacob throws himself directly on God's promise by a night of prayer, first in quietude and calmness, and then when the stillness, the loneliness and the darkness of the night are upon him, he makes the all-night wrestling prayer.

'With thee I mean all night to stay, And wrestle till the break of day.'

God's being is involved, His promise is at stake, and much is involved in the issue. Esau's temper, his conduct and his character are involved. It is a notable occasion. Much depends upon it. Jacob pursues his case and presses his plea with great struggles and hard wrestling. it is the highest form of importunity. But the victory is gained at last. His name and nature are changed and he becomes a new and different man. Jacob himself is saved first of all. He is blessed in his life and soul. But more still is accomplished. Esau undergoes a radical change of mind. He who came forth with hate and revenge in his heart against his own brother, seeking Jacob's destruction, is strangely and wonderfully affected, and he is changed and his whole attitude toward his brother becomes radically different. And when the two brothers meet, love takes the place of fear and hate, and they vie with each other in showing true brotherly affection.

The promise of God is fulfilled. But it took that all night of importunate praying to do the deed. It took that fearful night of wrestling on Jacob's part of make the promise sure and cause it to bear fruit. Prayer wrought the marvellous deed. So prayer of the same kind will produce like results in this day. It was God's promise and Jacob's praying which crowned and crowded the results so wondrously.

'Go show thyself to Ahab and I will send rain on the earth,' was God's command and promise to His servant Elijah after the sore famine had cursed the land. Many glorious results marked that day of heroic faith and dauntless courage on Elijah's part. The sublime issue with Israel had been successful, the fire had fallen, Israel had been reclaimed, the prophets of Baal had been killed, but there was no rain. The one thing, the only thing, which God had promised, had not been given. The day was declining, and the awestruck crowds were faint, and yet held by an invisible hand.

Elijah turns from Israel to God and from Baal to the one source of help for a final issue and a final victory. But seven times is the restless eagerness of the prophet stayed. Not till the seventh repeated time is his vigilance rewarded and the promise pressed to its final fulfilment. Elijah's fiery, relentless praying bore to its triumphant results the promise of God, and rain descended in full showers.

> Thy promise, Lord, is ever sure,
> And they that in Thy house would dwell
> That happy station to secure,
> Must still in holiness excel.

OUR PRAYERS ARE TOO FEEBLE

Our prayers are too little and too feeble to execute the purposes or to claim the promises of God with appropriating power. Marvellous purposes need marvellous praying to execute them. Miracle-making promises need miracle-making praying to realise them. Only Divine praying can operate Divine promises or carry out Divine purposes. How great, how sublime, and how exalted are the promises God makes to His people! How eternal are the purposes of God!

Why are we so impoverished in experience and so low in life when God's promises are so 'exceeding great and precious'? Why do the eternal purposes of God more so tardily? Why are they so poorly executed? Our failure to appropriate the Divine promises and rest our faith on them, and to pray believing is the solution. 'We have not because we ask not.' We ask and receive not because we ask amiss.'

Prayer is based on the purpose and promise of God. Prayer is submission to God. Prayer has no sigh of disloyalty against God's will. It may cry out against the bitterness and the dread weight of an hour of unutterable anguish: 'If it be possible, let this cup pass from me.' But it is surcharged with the sweetest and promptest submission. 'Yet not my will, but thine be done.'

THE SURE FOUNDATION OF PRAYER

But prayer in its usual uniform and deep current is conscious conformity to God's will, based upon the direct promise of God's Word, and under the illumination and application of the Holy Spirit. Nothing is surer than that the Word of God is the sure foundation of prayer. We pray just as we believe God's Word. Prayer is based directly and specifically upon God's revealed promises in Christ Jesus. It has no other ground upon which to base its plea. All else is shadowy, sandy, fickle. Not our feelings, not our merits, not our works, but God's promise is the basis of faith and the solid ground of prayer.

Now I have found the ground wherein
Sure my soul's anchor may remain;
The wounds of Jesus - for my sin,
Before the world's foundation slain.

The converse of this proposition is also true. God's promises are dependent and conditioned upon prayer to appropriate them and make them a conscious realisation. The promises are inwrought in us, appropriated by us, and held in the arms of faith in prayer. Let it be noted that prayer gives the promises in their efficiency, localises and appropriates them, and utilises them. Prayer puts the promises as the seed in the fructifying soil. Promises, like the rain, are general. Prayer embodies, precipitates, and locates them for personal use. Prayer goes by faith into the great fruit orchard of God's exceeding great promises, and with hand and heart picks the ripest and richest fruit. The promises, like electricity, may sparkle and dazzle and yet be impotent for good till these dynamic, life-giving currents are chained by prayer, and are made the mighty forces which move and bless.

Postscript

Prayer is not monologue, but dialogue: God's voice in response to mine is its most essential part. Listening to God's voice is the secret of the assurance that he will listen to mine.

Andrew Murray

Many people pray for things that can only come by work and work for things that can only come by prayer.

W. E. Sangster

We need less travelling by jet planes from congress to congress ... but more kneeling and praying and pleading to God to have mercy upon us, more crying to God to arise and scatter His enemies and make Himself known.

D. Martin Lloyd-Jones

The Christian on his knees sees more than the philosopher on tiptoe.

Augustus M. Toplady

I am only as tall as I am on my knees.
Stephen Olford

Prayer is often conceived to be little more than a technique for self-advancement, a heavenly method for achieving earthly success.
A. W. Tozer

Prayer is not something that I do: prayer is something that I am.
Warren Wiersbe

God is still on the throne, we're still on His footstool, and there's only a knee's distance between.
Jim Elliot

The self-sufficient do not pray, the self-satisfied will not pray, the self-righteous cannot pray.

Leonard Ravenhill

Prayer is a shield to the soul, a sacrifice to God and a scourge for Satan.

John Bunyan

I can take my telescope and look millions of miles into space: but I can go away to my room and in prayer get nearer to God and heaven than I can when assisted by all the telescopes of earth.

Isaac Newton

Much of our praying is just asking God to bless some folks that are ill, and to keep us plugging along. But prayer is not merely prattle, it is warfare.

Alan Redpath

Most Christians expect little from God, ask little and therefore receive little and are content with little.

A. W. Pink

I seldom made an errand to God for another but I got something for myself.

Samuel Rutherford

As air is the breath of life, so prayer is the breath of faith.

Paul Yonggi Cho

Let us see God before man every day.

Robert Murray McCheyne